My Advent Journal

My Advent Journal

A SPIRITUAL JOURNEY TO CHRISTMAS

WILLIAM F. MAESTRI

ALBA · HOUSE   NEW · YORK
SOCIETY OF ST. PAUL, 2187 VICTORY BLVD., STATEN ISLAND, NY 10314

Designed and produced in the United States of
America by the Fathers and Brothers of the
Society of St. Paul, 2187 Victory Boulevard,
Staten Island, New York 10314, as part of their
communications apostolate.

ISBN: 0-8189-0599-9

© *Copyright 1990 by the Society of St. Paul*

Printing Information:

Current Printing - first digit   1 2 3 4 5 6 7

Year of Current Printing - first year shown

1990   1991   1992   1993   1994   1995   1996   1997

CONTENTS

Introduction / vii

I. ISAIAH: WAITING IN HOPE

First Sunday of Advent: The hiddenness of God / 3
Monday of the First Week of Advent: Walk in the light of the Lord / 6
Tuesday of the First Week of Advent:
    Blest are the eyes that see what you see / 9
Wednesday of the First Week of Advent: He will destroy the veil / 12
Thursday of the First Week of Advent: The footsteps of the poor / 15
Friday of the First Week of Advent: Are you confident I can do this? / 18
Saturday of the First Week of Advent: No more will you weep / 21

II. JOHN THE BAPTIZER: A HERALD'S VOICE

Second Sunday of Advent: Make ready the way of the Lord / 26
Monday of the Second Week of Advent: He comes to save you / 28
Tuesday of the Second Week of Advent: In search of the stray / 31
Wednesday of the Second Week of Advent: Have you not heard? / 34
Thursday of the Second Week of Advent: A man called John / 37
Friday of the Second Week of Advent: He is mad! / 40
Saturday of the Second Week of Advent: Suffer at their hands / 43

III. PAUL: THE MYSTERY OF GOD'S LOVE

Third Sunday of Advent: Rejoice always / 48
Monday of the Third Week of Advent: On what authority? / 50
Tuesday of the Third Week of Advent: I will leave a remnant / 53
Wednesday of the Third Week of Advent: Let justice also spring up / 56
Thursday of the Third Week of Advent: Enduring love / 59
Friday of the Third Week of Advent: Loving the name of the Lord / 62

IV. MARY: THE MOTHERLY LOVE OF GOD

Fourth Sunday of Advent: Blessed are you among women / 66
December 17: The family record of Jesus / 68
December 18: The Lord our justice / 71
December 19: True in due season / 74
December 20: She was deeply troubled / 77
December 21: Renew you in His love / 80
December 22: Mary remained with Elizabeth / 83
December 23: Friendship with the Lord / 86
December 24: The way of peace / 89

CHRISTMAS: *Jesus: The Word Made Flesh* / 92

Advent notes and thoughts / 94

INTRODUCTION

Advent is a short season long on opportunity for spiritual growth. These four quickly-moving weeks bring into sharp focus the story of God's limitless love for us. The Spirit stirs within our hearts during this season of grace with its hope of new life and rebirth. We long to cry out the words of the Fourth Gospel: "And the Word was made flesh and dwelt among us, full of grace and truth; we have beheld His glory, the glory of the only Son coming from the Father" (Jn 1:14). Yet before we can make these words our own, we must dwell in the tension that comes to all who wait in hope. Before we can proclaim the Word as flesh we must live the words of Isaiah: "Prepare the way of the Lord, make his paths straight — a highway for our God" (Is 40:3). These four weeks of Advent are about preparing our hearts, and the whole of God's creation, for the coming of the Word in our poor flesh.

The short season of Advent is not the sentimental season so often commercialized by our society. Even less is Advent the season of a romantic Christianity which ignores the deeper, more demanding aspects of God coming into our hearts and history. Advent is the story of God's total, never-ending commitment to us. Such a commitment in love always comes at a high price. St. Paul writing to the Philippians powerfully captures the cost of love: "... though in the form of God, He did not count equality with God a thing to be grasped, but emptied himself, taking the form of a servant, being born in the likeness of men" (Ph 2:6-7). Such a divine love calls for a response from the human heart. We are challenged to empty ourselves of all those things which keep the Word from taking on flesh in our hearts. This emptying of ourselves requires that we die to the old self so as to be born anew. In fact, the only way the Word can be enfleshed in us is to be emptied of our illusions of self-sufficiency, total control, and the influence of our power. Once we let go of these false securities, the Word can be born in us with all its power to liberate and transform.

The power of the season of Advent can be found in its major themes and disclosure models. The child in the crib, the mother beholding her son, and the gathering of shepherds speak to us of the boundless, faithful, tender and life-giving love of God. The Christmas story of Luke tells us that God comes offering, not the love of power, but the power of love. God does not come to condemn but to heal and to offer us the opportunity to begin again. No matter what our past, we are offered a future to hope in and a God to love, not fear. The Christmas story invites us to live in such a way that hope is stronger than despair; grace abounds more than sin; light overcomes the darkness; and love conquers even death.

Father Andrew Greeley, in his book *The Catholic Myth*, goes so far as to say that the Christmas story perfectly reveals the Catholic religious imagination. The Catholic community believes that God's grace is everywhere, most especially in the intimate relationships of the family circle: of husband, wife and children. The human love of husband and wife mirrors God's love for us. The passionate, tender love of a mother for her child reflects God's love for us. The Christmas story proclaims the grace of God at work transforming our hearts of stone into hearts of flesh. To know what God's love is all about, we must look to the crib; to Mary with her child.

Advent holds before us several towering figures of faith: Isaiah, John the Baptizer, Mary and St. Paul. These four ancestors in faith can be for our journey to Christmas what David Tracy calls disclosure models: historical individuals whose lives reveal profound and enduring truths about ourselves and our relationship to God and one another. They make known to us essential aspects of properly waiting for the Lord and reveal to us authentic ways in which we are always an Advent People, a people waiting in hope for the Lord to come and come again. These ancestors in faith share our humanity and show us what is possible through grace and the willingness to open our hearts to change. We share their story and hope their destiny will one day be ours.

The Advent season with its emphasis on waiting can easily be misunderstood. To wait is not to be passive, inactive, and inattentive. Waiting for the Lord requires an alertness, sobriety and urgent longing. To properly wait requires that we engage life. Advent is not a call to withdraw and let God do it all. Advent challenges us to live more deeply the love of God and to be more sensitive to the rumor of angels and the signals of transcendence which surround us daily.

My Advent Journal has as one of its goals the stirring of the heart and the sharpening of one's vision. We can do this by prayerfully reflecting on our spiritual journey to Christmas. It is so easy to forget the deeper meaning of this joyful season of God's visitation, His incarnation. By spending a few minutes reading Scripture, prayerfully reflecting on God's Word, and thoughtfully writing about our faith journey we will be drawn into the mystery of the Word made flesh.

The structure of this Journal is eminently simple. There are four major sections corresponding to the four weeks of Advent. Section five, which brings the Journal to a close, centers on Jesus, the Word of God Incarnate. Each section opens with a Sunday reflection and conversation with one of our leading Advent disclosure models: Isaiah, John the Baptizer, St. Paul and Mary. After each Sunday, the weekdays of Advent follow. For each there is a citation of the biblical reading with a brief explanation of the theme. After you read the daily Scripture selections, spend a few minutes in quiet reflection. Now write your responses to the questions and statements. A short meditation is presented based on the biblical readings and an appropriate aspect of the Advent journey. A brief closing conversation/ reflection concludes each section. At the end of Advent you will have entered into dialogue with the major disclosure models of this grace-filled season and grown in love for the Lord who comes. You will have composed an important chapter in your personal journey and will be ready to greet the King of kings. You will not have spent this holy season in vain, for when the Christmas angel proclaims the birth of the Messiah, the child Jesus will be born again in you.

I am grateful to Father Edmund and Brother Aloysius of the Society of St. Paul as well as the entire community of Staten Island. The gift of their friendship and faith keeps me going year round. The Benedictines of St. Joseph Abbey have taught me much about waiting in hope. This book is dedicated to Abbot Patrick Regan, O.S.B. who has been my professor and continues to be my friend.

William F. Maestri
St. Joseph Abbey
St. Benedict, Louisiana

*T*he only way in which man can have peace
is to accept the incomprehensible God in the incomprehensibility of
our existence and lot. But one can only accept both of these because
God himself has accepted
us when he himself came in the inward conflict of our own flesh.
Would not the beginning of eternal
peace be there if at Christmas we were to say a
quiet 'Yes' to God who came, accepted us, divided and broken though
we were, and in his
own person brought us reconciliation and unity?

—*Karl Rahner "Peace on Earth"*

I. ISAIAH: WAITING IN HOPE

To be modern is to be in a hurry. We don't like to wait. We think that getting what we want when we want it is part of our natural rights. At times we are even willing to overlook quality as long as we get what we desire fast. We crave the instant; from fast foods to the latest fad in spirituality, we look for the quick fix. Yet in our more reflective moments we know the importance of time and the wisdom of those who know how to wait for the unfolding of truth, beauty, and goodness.

The prophet never looks for quick results or instant conversion. In fact, the prophet knows how resistant the human heart is to change. The great Hebrew prophet of Advent, Isaiah, is a messenger who calls us to wait in patient hope. Such a hope does not demand immediate results. Patient hope is the willingness to live with the tension of the God who is here and beyond; in our midst and yet transcends our world. The voice of Isaiah reaches out to us across the centuries with words of encouragement: "The Lord is near; do not despair."

The prophet Isaiah challenges us to overcome our fear of disappointment in waiting for one who comes not. The Lord will never forget his covenant. The Lord never goes back on His word. The Lord is near. Do you not perceive Him? Do you not hear His voice?

Sunday OF THE FIRST WEEK

The hiddenness of God

How strange it seems to begin a new liturgical year, and the season of Advent, by reflecting on the hiddenness of God. After all, shouldn't we be poised and ready for the coming of the Christ Child? If ever there was a season in which the presence of the Lord is felt, Advent would certainly be that season.

However the prophet Isaiah knows well how easily distracted we human beings are. Parties, packages, and bright lights can easily turn us away from the true meaning of this season. On a much deeper level, we become increasingly aware, especially during Advent, how much our world and heart lack peace. The reality of sin, with its power to alienate and divide, becomes more present during this season of grace. We become aware of our need for healing. Rather than the presence of God in our midst, we feel more deeply His absence. We know the need for God from the ache which reminds us of how much we have lost our way.

Toward the end of the book of Isaiah (read chapters 63 and 64), we find this poet and mystic pleading for the Lord to return: "Oh, that you would rend the heavens and come down, with the mountains quaking before you... awesome deeds we could not hope for" (Is 63:19ff). Isaiah is speaking on behalf of a people in exile. They have broken the covenant by worshiping false gods, seeking security in military alliances, and ignoring the demands of social justice. The Lord has left them in their sin and allowed them to be prisoners of their guilt. The prophet is praying for deliverance. The mighty God of Exodus can once again come to save His people; not from Pharaoh, but from themselves.

The black picture painted by Isaiah turns to hope and confidence in God: "Yet, O Lord, you are our father; we are the clay and you are the potter: we are all the work of your hands" (Is 64:8). Even though the Lord is hidden because of our sinfulness, He has not abandoned us. The prophet is confident that the Lord will never forget the people He has lovingly fashioned for Himself. We see at work a story of God older than Exodus, namely the God of Genesis, who lovingly forms us and breathes His very life-breath into us. The hiddenness of God is in reality our movement away from Him through sin. It is we who have hidden from God and broken the covenant. The Lord is always ready to return so we may be healed. The Lord is always near. It is we who must stop fleeing from God.

The prophet prays that the Lord will return with displays of power: rending the heavens, causing the mountains to quake, and performing mighty deeds of deliverance such as those he performed when the Israelites were brought out of Egypt. Maybe if the Lord were to impress us, or frighten us with His power, we will return to the covenant. Yet we know that the Lord's ways are not our own. He will come to save His people, but not surrounded by the trappings of power and divine might. The Lord will come hidden in the presence of a little child, born to a woman under the law, and will totally assume the poverty of our human condition.

The season of Advent challenges us to see the hidden presence of God. He is not to be found among the rich and famous, but with the lowly and humble of heart. The Lord does not want us to fear Him but to love Him in response to His having loved us first. During this season we cry, "Come Lord Jesus," and the Word made flesh responds, "Behold, I am in your midst. The time of salvation is at hand."

Reflection Questions Read the following passages from the prophet Isaiah: 63:16-17, 19; 64:2-7; 2:1-5; and 61:1-2, 10-12. Prayerfully reflect on these readings. Write a brief response to the following questions on these Advent readings.

In what ways have I broken covenant relationship with the Lord?

___

___

___

How have I experienced the love of God in my life? How have I shared that love with others?

___

___

___

How do I experience the hiddenness of God?

___

___

How have I worked for peace in my daily life?

_____

_____

_____

_____

Closing Conversation. In the following section allow yourself to enter into a prayerful conversation with Isaiah. Reflect on Isaiah's questions and write your responses.

Isaiah: How has sin caused the Lord to be hidden in your life?

Response: _____

_____

_____

_____

_____

Isaiah: In what ways are you seeking reconciliation with the Lord?

Response: _____

_____

_____

_____

_____

Isaiah: How are you helping others to come to the Lord for healing?

Response: _____

_____

_____

_____

_____

Monday OF THE FIRST WEEK

Isaiah 2:1-5 The Lord is the Lord of all and desires that the peoples of the earth come to dwell on His holy mountain. The barriers of race, culture, and nationality will be overcome. The prophet offers a vision of peace through obedience to the Lord's will.

Isaiah 4:2-6 (Year A) All who remain faithful to the Lord will find deliverance and comfort. God never abandons His people or forgets His promises. The Lord will come and wash away His people's sins.

Matthew 8:5-11 Jesus comes into our human condition to heal us of sin and restore us to health. Yet we must look to Jesus with a confident faith. The words of Jesus are filled with power to heal.

Walk in the Light of the Lord

At this time of the year we are surrounded by sights: lights from Christmas trees, residential and business decorations, and even the traffic lights take on a seasonal luster. Unfortunately many of these lights quickly burn out or simply get put away when Christmas ends. Such temporary lights burn brightly but they cannot serve us in all the seasons of our life. We must find that one Light that is lasting and true.

The prophet Isaiah tells us that only the Lord is such a light. Too often the peoples of the earth have tried to light their way by trusting their swords, spears and military alliances. These false lights, however, have produced only heat and further divided the family of God. Still others have looked for truth and security in material possessions only to be left disappointed and empty.

Where is one to go for that light which endures through a lifetime and beyond? Amidst all the contrary lights that surround us, where are we to find the Light of Life? The prophet Isaiah provides the answer: "Let us walk in the light of the Lord!" It is only in obeying the loving will of God, revealed in the covenant and in the person of Jesus, that we come into the Light of Life.

It is not enough that we dwell in the light and seek the way of the Lord. We are sent forth to share the Lord's wisdom with others, for the instruction of the Lord holds out the only true hope for lasting peace: "They shall beat their swords into plowshares and their spears into pruning hooks." This time of Advent calls for us to walk in the light of the Lord and bring that light of truth to the world we touch. In so doing we are helping to extend the Lord's kingdom of justice, freedom and peace.

Reflection Questions. The mountain of the Lord is a symbol for His dwelling place. It will also serve as the home for all the peoples of the earth. The Lord comes not for the few but for all who desire peace.

In what ways am I preparing for the coming of Jesus?

How have I helped others to know the Lord?

How can I help my local parish be a place of peace for the larger community?

Advent is a season of faith in the promises of God. The Lord comes to heal us. He has power, not only to heal our souls but to supply us with the grace to be physically whole or to accept our sufferings as a grace.

How have I experienced the Lord's healing power?

8 MY ADVENT JOURNAL

How have I been an instrument of God's healing love for others?

_____
_____
_____
_____

Closing Conversation. Read today's Gospel prayerfully and spend a few minutes in silent reflection. Write your response to Jesus' question.

Jesus: What healing, for yourself or another, do you hope to experience during this Advent season?

Response: _____

_____
_____
_____
_____
_____
_____
_____
_____
_____
_____
_____
_____
_____
_____
_____
_____
_____
_____
_____

Tuesday OF THE FIRST WEEK

Isaiah 11:1-10 The Lord sends the Spirit into our hearts with the gifts of wisdom, understanding, counsel, strength, knowledge, and fear of the Lord. These gifts are for all God's peoples: Jew and Gentile. We are to wait in hope for such a time of the Spirit.

Luke 10:21-24 The mysteries of the Kingdom do not come to the learned, clever or powerful. Jesus reveals the will of the Father to all who are willing to accept His teachings in child-like faith and trust. Happy are those who are able to see and hear Jesus as the Son of God.

Blest are the eyes that see what you see

So much of our daily life requires that we see properly. The precious gift of sight is necessary for driving a car to catching a glimpse of an approaching friend. Great fear grips us if we receive word from the doctor that our sight is in danger of being lost. No longer would our sight help us to thrill at the sunrise of a new day or feel the mysterious peace of the velvet night.

The eyes are the windows to the soul and we are concerned about sight enriched by faith which leads to insight. Growth in the spiritual life is the grace to move from the visible to the invisible; the material to the spiritual. In the words of Isaiah: "Not by appearance shall He judge...." The Lord searches our hearts and sees where no human love can penetrate. We need not fear having the Lord know our inmost thoughts, for the Lord searches our inmost being with the light of love. The Lord does not come to condemn us but to heal us of sin and offer us a new way of living.

The gift of the Holy Spirit helps us to see the presence of God all around us. The Spirit helps us to look beyond appearances and not judge others by what we immediately see or feel. Faith helps us to look deeper. We are blest if we can look at the crib and see the Word made flesh. We are blest if we can hear the Gospel and put it into practice. The blessings of this season do not depend on our moral goodness or worldly achievements. The coming of God into our humanity and the preaching of the Gospel results from the gracious will of our loving God.

MY ADVENT JOURNAL

Reflection Questions. There can be no real peace without justice. An essential part of the covenant with Yahweh is care for the poor and working to reform sinful social structures. Only with justice can there be reconciliation.

In what ways have I worked for justice?

_____
_____
_____
_____

How have I helped the poor and worked to build a more just society?

_____
_____
_____
_____

How have I been an instrument of the Lord's reconciliation in my family and parish?

_____
_____
_____
_____

Jesus comes to do the will of the Father. Essential to Jesus' mission is telling us of the Father's love for us. Happy are those who accept Jesus and the Gospel.

What gifts of the Holy Spirit do I most need?

_____
_____
_____
_____

Do I find myself judging others by appearances? _____ Why? _____

In what ways have I rejoiced in the Holy Spirit?

Closing Conversation. Allow yourself to enter into prayerful conversation with Jesus. After reflecting on Jesus' questions, write your own responses.

Jesus: Are you open to receive the mysteries of the Kingdom in faith?

Response: _____

Jesus: What are the major obstacles which keep you from seeing me as the Son of God?

Response: _____

Jesus: How have you helped others to accept me and the Gospel?

Response: _____

Wednesday OF THE FIRST WEEK

Isaiah 25:6-10 The prophet turns our attention to that time when the Lord will come in full glory. It will be a time of abundance, recognition, and peace. We shall see God as He is and rejoice forever.

Matthew 15:29-37 Jesus is moved with pity at the sight of all who are in need of healing. Jesus' love always involves more than words. Jesus actively goes about healing and feeding the crowd.

He will destroy the veil

Advent is the season for uncovering and bringing to light the mystery of God's boundless love for all peoples. Yet we know that such an uncovering is still a hope rather than a present reality. The veil that divides humankind, and the human heart, is still very much with us. Nations still prepare for war as they talk about peace. People kill one another in the name of religion and the stranger is still treated with fear and mistrust. There is a growing violence in our families, and within our hearts we can feel alienated and at odds on account of the good we desire and the evil we give in to.

Our newspapers illustrate the many ways in which this veil divides us. Isaiah, though, in today's Scripture passage, reassures us: "On this mountain He will destroy the veil that veils all peoples." The veil that divides us and lies behind the increasing violence in society was never a part of God's plan for His creation. It is the result of sin which hides our common humanity and makes us forget that we are members of one family of God. The words of Isaiah give us reason to hope.

What is it that will remove the veil that divides us? It is the very love of God made visible in the child Jesus. It is the very compassion of God taking on our human life that gives us the hope for that time when "the Lord will wipe away the tears from all faces." This love of God made visible in Jesus has been entrusted to us. We are to continue to help remove that veil which divides people. We do this by feeding the hungry, caring for the sick, and helping to build bridges of understanding. In doing these things we help lift the veil so the glory of God can shine through.

Reflection Questions. All of our heart's desires will be satisfied on the Lord's mountain. And what we most long for is the peace that comes from dwelling in the Lord's presence with the family of humankind. At the Eucharist we anticipate the eternal banquet of salvation.

What do I most need in my preparation for the Lord's coming?

What specific actions have I taken to be reconciled with my enemies?

In what ways have I tried to promote understanding among different peoples?

Jesus is the compassion of God made visible in our midst. Jesus does not simply go about the work of healing; He is "moved to pity" at the needs of the people. Jesus enters into our humanity so as to bring us healing and life.

What works of mercy have I performed in imitation of Jesus?

Do I find myself a compassionate person, especially toward the poor? _____ In what way?

How do I share myself and my abundance with others?

Closing Conversation. Reflect on the following questions and, after a prayerful conversation with Jesus, write your responses.

Jesus: Do you believe that I have the power to cure you in body and soul?

Response

Jesus: Are you able to give thanks for the gifts you received and share them with others?

Response:

Jesus: Have you developed a devotion to the Blessed Sacrament as a source of strength? How?

Response

Thursday OF THE FIRST WEEK

Isaiah 26:1-6 The cities of Judah have broken their covenant with the Lord. The result is defeat and exile. Their only hope is to trust in the Lord who will hear their prayers and form a remnant. The remnant will do justice and seek the Lord's will.

Matthew 7:21, 24-27 Jesus reminds us that words are never enough. There must always be action if we are to build a sound foundation for our faith. If we only rely on words, our faith is never tested nor is it strengthened.

The footsteps of the poor

No society celebrates its poor or promotes its declining standard of material living. We want to let everyone know about the rich and famous who live among us. We beat our collective chest in telling the world we have the highest standard of material comfort. Nations often judge their worth in terms of the GNP (Gross National Product). However, it is easy to forget about the poor. We try our best to render invisible those who have not kept pace in acquiring wealth. The poor come to count for nothing. They become non-persons and are given no respect.

The prophet Isaiah reminds the people (and us as well) that the material well-being of a society is never secured if the moral health of that society is ignored. And we cannot be morally healthy if we trample the poor underfoot and turn our backs on the needs of those who are hurting, powerless, and without resources. Only a nation which respects the demands of social justice will be in covenant with the Lord. Only a nation which does justice will know lasting peace. Those who are entrusted with authority must never forget their primary work is to lead the community into the way of the Lord and establish justice within the city. No faith community can truly claim to seek the Lord all the while forgetting the needy.

Jesus tells us that words, while necessary, are never sufficient for the true life of faith. It is not enough to preach and talk about the Gospel, we must put our words into action. Without action our spiritual life is just sentiment or some kind of romantic image which avoids the challenges of real life. The solid life of faith requires both words and deeds. Advent reminds us that the Word became flesh. Jesus did not merely become human. He actively went about caring for the sick and the poor. And we are expected to do the same.

16 MY ADVENT JOURNAL

Reflection Questions. The only one deserving of our total trust is the Lord. The proud trust in their riches, powerful positions and military strength. When the Lord comes, however, the mighty will be humbled and the humble will be exalted.

In what ways do I see my nation trusting in the Lord?

___

___

___

___

Turning away?

___

___

___

___

How have I failed to trust in the Lord by seeking security in possessions?

___

___

___

___

Jesus reminds us that the Christian life calls for sacrifice and a willingness to face trials. Following Jesus does not mean that we are excused from the cross. However, no trial will destroy us if we have faith in Jesus.

What trials have I faced recently in witnessing to my faith?

___

___

___

___

___

THURSDAY OF THE FIRST WEEK 17

How have I helped others face the storms of life with trust in Jesus?

_____

_____

_____

_____

In what ways have I just talked about my faith instead of putting it into practice?

_____

_____

_____

_____

Closing Conversation. Meditate on the parable of Jesus from our Gospel reading. Write your response to Jesus.

Jesus: Tell me of one of your major crises of faith. How did trust in the loving will of the Father give you the necessary strength to persevere?

Response: _____

_____

_____

_____

_____

_____

_____

_____

_____

_____

_____

Friday OF THE FIRST WEEK

Isaiah 29:17-24 The coming of the Messiah will establish the reign of God. The Lord's rule will be characterized by freedom, justice, and peace. Those who have abused the poor and mistreated the weak will be driven away from the Lord.

Matthew 9:27-31 An essential aspect of Jesus' ministry is healing. Two blind men are cured. However, Jesus reminds them that such a cure requires faith. It is faith in Jesus that brings us from darkness to light.

Are you confident I can do this?

In recent years we have witnessed a decline in confidence in our major institutions. From Wall Street to Washington we have witnessed various scandals and abuses of power. It is easy to become cynical and lose faith with those who have been entrusted with promoting the common good. Organized religion has not escaped this present loss of confidence. We have trusted various religious personalities who have abused that trust. Some have even gone to jail for taking money and using church funds to support an extravagant lifestyle. It's not surprising that many have lost confidence in religion and its leaders.

The question of Jesus in our Gospel is more timely than ever, "Are you confident I can do this?" The blind men answer "Yes" and are cured. It is important to remember what Jesus tells these men: "Because of your faith it shall be done to you." Jesus is not a magician who tries to impress people with His power. His ministry of healing is a sign of the Kingdom of God in the midst of the people. Healing is never an end in itself but always points to the loving will of the Father. Jesus comes to do the will of the Father. He continually rejects all attempts to make Him king or a worldly leader. Jesus is the compassion of God made visible in a stable. Jesus is the unbounded love of God made visible on the cross. The crib and the cross point us to see, with the eyes of faith, the God who loves us.

The men who are cured cannot contain their joy. They go about telling everyone what the Lord had done for them. Jesus continues to heal us through the indwelling Holy Spirit. We are to go about telling the story of God's love which has made us whole.

Reflection Questions. We can never judge the outcome of our lives or human history by looking only at the present moment. We are to be a people of hope. Even in the midst of pain and tragedy God is at work.

How do I spiritually cope with the evil I suffer?

_____

_____

_____

_____

How have I spiritually confronted evil in my own soul?

_____

_____

_____

_____

Have I opened myself to God's grace through the sacrament of Reconciliation? Have I found peace through Confession?

_____

_____

_____

_____

The healing ministry of Jesus requires faith on our part. We must open our hearts to receive Jesus as Lord. If we come to Jesus without childlike faith we remain in the dark.

In what ways has my faith been tested? How have I responded?

_____

_____

_____

_____

_____

20 MY ADVENT JOURNAL

In what ways have I been blind to Jesus working in my life?

How have I witnessed to others so they may come to Jesus in faith?

Closing Conversation. Reflect on our Gospel reading. After spending some time in prayer write your responses to Jesus.

Jesus: Are you confident I can heal you?

Response: _____

Jesus: Is your faith childlike enough to accept your healing?

Response: _____

Jesus: How can I help you grow in faith?

Response: _____

Saturday OF THE FIRST WEEK

Isaiah 30:19-21, 23-26 What a beautiful picture Isaiah presents concerning the coming of the Lord! It will be a time when all weeping, suffering and division will be overcome. The Lord will dwell with His people. It will be a time of abundance.

Matthew 9:35-10:1, 6-8 The central theme of Jesus' preaching is the good news of God's reign. The reign of God is not just something we receive but a gift we must share.

No more will you weep

The prophet Isaiah is given a tough task: he must speak a word of hope to a people in exile. The Israelites have wandered from the ways of the covenant. They no longer wish to trust the Lord and walk in the ways of social justice. The result is tragic. The Israelites are in bondage in a foreign land. Once again they find themselves under the yoke of slavery by a strange power: Babylon. When will their deliverance come?

Isaiah's words of hope also contain a word of hard realism. Israel is in bondage because it has deserted the Lord. The Lord has not abandoned His people; it is Israel who has gone in search of security based on earthly powers. Israel is not like other nations. Israel is special to the Lord. Yet the covenant comes with responsibilities. Yahweh alone is to be their security and the mighty waters of social justice must be flowing among the people.

When the people turn from sin and seek the Lord, He is to be found. The Lord does not force Himself into our lives. It is up to us to turn from sin. When we come to our senses we find that the Lord has been there all the while. The Lord, too, waits in patience for us. His love is strong enough to wait us out and His love is tender enough to welcome us home with compassion. When we finally turn back to the Lord, often bitter and fearful, what do we find? Isaiah tells us: "On the day the Lord binds up the wounds of His people, He will heal the bruises left by His blows."

MY ADVENT JOURNAL

Reflection Questions. The Lord is the good and true shepherd of His people. It is the Lord who formed Israel as a people. It is the Lord who brought them out of bondage into freedom. When the people turn from sin to the Lord they find abundant blessings.

In what ways do I support religious leaders in teaching God's word?

_____
_____
_____
_____

In what ways do I support civic leaders in working for the common good?

_____
_____
_____
_____

How have I rebelled against authority because of pride?

_____
_____
_____
_____

Jesus is the true Teacher spoken of in Isaiah. The will of God is revealed in the person and teaching of Jesus. Jesus reveals to all who see with faith the way that leads to eternal life.

In what ways have I been moved to pity and help the sick and poor?

_____
_____
_____
_____
_____
_____

SATURDAY OF THE FIRST WEEK

How have I shared the gift of my faith with others?

_____
_____
_____

In what ways can I help the sick in hospitals and those who care for them?

_____
_____
_____

Closing Conversation. Spend a few minutes in prayer reflecting on our Gospel. Write your response to Jesus.

Jesus: How have you shared in witnessing to the Kingdom at work or school?

Response:

_____
_____
_____

Jesus: Do you put your faith into practice by giving alms to the poor?

Response:

_____
_____
_____

Jesus: What is the one gift you want to share with others? Do you?

Response:

_____
_____
_____
_____

II. JOHN THE BAPTIZER: A HERALD'S VOICE

The second week of Advent turns our attention from the Hebrew prophet Isaiah to the voice of one crying in the wilderness, John the Baptizer. At first look, John does not seem to fit in very well with our Advent sentiments. The air is filled with talk of reconciliation, peace, unity, and the coming of the child Jesus. For the past week we have been captivated with the beautiful poetry of Isaiah's vision of the coming of the Lord: wolf and lamb will be friends; the Gentiles shall come to dwell on the Lord's mountain; there will be a feast of rich foods and choice wines; tears and suffering will be banished; and the Lord will reveal Himself to all the peoples of the earth. With the coming of John we turn from a poetic vision of what will be to the present demands of conversion as the coming of the Lord draws near.

John the Baptizer is a much needed corrective to the overly sentimental approach to Christmas. John is an enormously fascinating figure. His very presence is redolent of mystery and the spiritual dimension of existence. John certainly doesn't dress the part of a respectable religious leader. He wears animal skins and eats the strangest foods: grasshoppers and wild honey. He avoids strong drink but not strong words, especially for the self-righteous and religiously respectable folks. John is God's man who announces the time of deliverance. The Kingdom of God is near at hand. It is not a time for complacency or smugness. It is a time for conversion and a change of heart. We can no longer live in the same old ways, guided by the same old values.

Advent is not the season to be jolly but joyful. The joy of this season comes from the Holy Spirit preparing our hearts to receive the birth of the Messiah. Conversion is never easy and change always calls for sacrifice. However, even in the midst of giving up the old securities we have the hope of a new beginning. The herald's voice is calling us to reform. The Lord is very near!

Sunday OF THE SECOND WEEK

Make ready the way of the Lord

One of the most difficult jobs in the fields of entertainment and politics is that of the "advance man." This person is expected to prepare the audience for the real star of the show. In politics, the advance man arrives weeks before the candidate. He or she is to prepare the local community by getting out press releases, setting up a headquarters, organizing volunteers for the campaign, and doing whatever it takes to insure a rousing welcome for the candidate. Many an election, as well as many an evening of entertainment, is determined by how well the advance man does his job. What is crucial is that the advance person does not take the light away from the star or the soon-to-arrive candidate. A good advance man must have a strong ego and know how to play his role. No doubt some advance men hope to headline the show themselves one day or run for political office.

John the Baptizer is Jesus' advance man. It is John who came as the one given the mission to herald the coming of the Messiah; and his coming is near at hand. John is a rather strange herald by modern standards. Few entertainers or politicians would want John as their advance man. He doesn't dress properly (camel's hair and a leather belt!) and his diet is not quite gourmet (grasshoppers and wild honey!). Above all, John does not come to comfort the troubled but rather to trouble the comfortable. In other words, John is perfect for the role of herald. He announces the coming of the Messiah. He knows he is not the Messiah. His baptism is with water. There is One coming who will baptize with the Spirit.

The ministry of John and his character reveal not only truths about Advent and Christmas but about the essence of what it means to be a Christian and a community of faith. Heralding the coming of Jesus is not just for four weeks. It is a life-long vocation. Heralding the Messiah is not just for the individual believer but for the Church as a whole. We not only proclaim the coming of the Lord in Bethlehem, we herald the Lord who will come again in glory. Advent not only turns our attention back to the stable, Advent calls us forward to that time when all hearts will be ready to receive the Lord. Until then we continue the ministry of John. In our own day and place we help make ready the coming of the Lord.

SUNDAY OF THE SECOND WEEK

Closing Conversation. Spend a few minutes in quiet prayer. Meditate on the ministry of John the Baptizer. Consider the many challenges that he faced in preparing the people for the coming of the Lord. Write your response to John's question.

John: How have you helped to prepare for the Lord's coming? How have you helped others? What obstacles have you faced? Have you overcome them?

Response: _____

Monday of the Second Week

Isaiah 35:1-10 Two great events influence Israel's history: the Exodus and the Exile. In both these events Yahweh is at work on behalf of the people though His ways are mysterious. At the end of the Exodus there is the Promised Land. At the end of the Exile there will be restoration.

Luke 5:17-26 Jesus continues the work of deliverance. This time it is not political bondage but the slavery of sin that Jesus confronts. The scribes and Pharisees accuse Jesus of blasphemy because they want the people to follow them and not God's way.

He comes to save you

Most of us do not look forward to visiting the doctor, especially the dentist. We fear the cure worse than the illness. It's amazing how the tooth stops aching and the pain leaves the body while we're waiting for the doctor to see us. We know that in order to be cured we often have to endure some suffering.

The prophet Isaiah tells the people that God is coming to save them. They need not fear. It will be a time of vindication, release, forgiveness, and restoration. Joy and gladness will abound. Sadness and suffering will finally cease to be. The earth will be full of the goodness of the Lord. This is quite a vision. Yet, in the back of minds, the nagging question persists, "What's it going to cost?"

Isaiah knows well the fear we face with the promise of every cure. Hence, the prophet writes, "Be strong, fear not!" Yes, salvation does cost us something. Yes, there is something we must do. In fact, we must do what we find most difficult: change! We must give up the old, sinful ways of pride, arrogance, and self-seeking. We must live as a people of the light who have been called to live as God's beloved. This is not easy. But the same Lord who calls us to salvation also provides the grace to accept the challenge.

No doubt the lame man in our Gospel was tempted to reject his cure. Life would have been so much easier on the mat. People would do things for him and excuse him from many of life's responsibilities. However, to remain on the mat would have been a refusal to grow as a human being. The paralysis would only become worse and eventually death would result.

Advent is a time when the Lord calls us to get off our mats and walk upright in His ways. We need not fear the cure. We can be strong in the Lord, for our God comes "with divine recompense to save us."

Reflection Questions. In times of prosperity the people of Israel tend to forget Yahweh and the covenant. The result of such forgetting is always tragic. Israel has been in exile. However, the prophet offers a vision of restoration.

How can our nation advance social justice?

_____
_____
_____
_____

How can our nation use its prosperity to help poorer countries?

_____
_____
_____
_____

How can our parish reach out to the poor and the sick?

_____
_____
_____
_____

Jesus comes to heal the people of their physical and moral infirmities. Not only does He cure the lame man but He says his sins are forgiven. The faith of the people stands in contrast to the hatred of the scribes and Pharisees.

Have I been afraid to accept healing from Jesus? Why?

_____
_____
_____
_____
_____
_____

30   MY ADVENT JOURNAL

Have I used illness or human weakness to be excused from daily responsibilities?

___

Have I helped others accept their healing from Jesus? How?

___

Closing Conversation.   Read the Gospel for today. Put yourself in place of the lame man. Write your response to the healing words of Jesus.

Jesus: I say to you, get up! Take up your mat... your sins are forgiven.

Response: ___

___

Jesus: Tell me of your fears about accepting your healing.

Response: ___

Tuesday OF THE SECOND WEEK

Isaiah 40:1-11 The prophet is often thought of as only proclaiming angry words about human sin and disobedience. However, the prophet also proclaims a word of comfort and deliverance. Isaiah is the prophet of hope. The Lord is near and the return home is close at hand.

Matthew 18:12-14 Jesus, the compassion of God, does not come to call the morally upright. He comes to search out those who have become lost and given up for dead. The Father desires that not one of His children ever be lost. The Father rejoices over all who repent.

In search of the stray

In our Gospel reading, Jesus poses an interesting question to His disciples: Does it make sense to leave ninety-nine sheep and go search after one which goes astray? This question seems so easy to answer. The response would appear to be obvious. To leave the ninety-nine in search of the one is foolish. No one in their right mind would risk losing the flock to search out one who decided to do its own thing. When the shepherd returned after looking for the one stray, no doubt many of the ninety-nine would have run off. Also, there is no guarantee that the one stray would be found or would want to return anyway. Imagine leaving the ninety-nine in search of the one and when you finally catch up with it, it refuses to return.

No doubt this easy and obvious answer strikes us as reasonable. Yet it is much to our benefit that our human wisdom is folly to God and God's folly is the wisdom and power which saves us. We are the strays that God the Father goes in search of. He sends the Son to seek out the lost with the good news of forgiveness, rebirth and unconditional acceptance. Jesus does not come to judge and condemn but to call all who are lost to come back home. The coming of Jesus is proof that God doesn't want anyone to be lost. Our heavenly Father risks our rejection and patiently waits for us to come to our senses and return. He also actively seeks us out with a word of forgiveness and understanding. And when any one of His children return there is unrestrained joy in heaven.

Advent is the season for celebrating the coming of the Word made flesh. Jesus tells us that heaven celebrates as well at the prospect of those who have gone astray returning to the Lord. Our heavenly Father wills that none of us remain distant from Him. Jesus leaves the ninety-nine and searches for us.

MY ADVENT JOURNAL

Reflection Questions. The Lord of Israel sends the prophet with words of comfort. The good news of deliverance is to be proclaimed. The Lord is the Good Shepherd who leads His people through the valley of death with care.

Do I experience the Lord's care through the sacraments, especially those of Reconciliation and the Eucharist?

_____
_____
_____
_____

Does my faith give me comfort in the face of death?

_____
_____
_____
_____

Do I pray for vocations to the priesthood? Do I pray for my parish priests?

_____
_____
_____
_____

Jesus tells us we are not sinners in the hands of an angry God but sinners lovingly accepted by a God who is our Father. He goes to endless lengths to seek us out for our salvation. Jesus is born in our hearts so that we might be reborn to new life.

How have I experienced the joy of the Holy Spirit through the forgiveness of my sins?

_____
_____
_____
_____
_____

TUESDAY OF THE SECOND WEEK

During this Advent season have I sought out those separated from the Church?

_____
_____
_____
_____

Can I rejoice when the sinner repents or do I feel resentful at God's mercy?

_____
_____
_____
_____
_____

Closing Conversation. Spend a few moments in quiet reflection reviewing the presence of sin in your life and the greater presence of God's grace. Write your responses to Jesus.

Jesus: Tell me of the ways you have strayed from our Father's home.

Response: _____
_____
_____
_____
_____

Jesus: What has been your greatest spiritual struggle?

Response: _____
_____
_____
_____
_____

Wednesday OF THE SECOND WEEK

Isaiah 40:25-31 The Lord of Israel is eternal, all powerful, and has brought all things into existence. Israelites must remember their dignity as God's people of the Covenant. When they forget the Lord, disaster results.

Matthew 11:28-30 Jesus does not come to burden us with the requirements of the law but He comes to free us through the power of grace. In the midst of our daily struggles, Jesus refreshes us and gives us the strength to follow Him every day.

Have you not heard?

Being in the know is a multi-billion dollar industry in America. Just walk through any supermarket and a dozen tabloids try to grab you with the alluring promise of the latest information on the rich and (in)famous. If you only buy this tabloid you will be in the know. You will be able to tell all your friends and club members about the latest exploits of those who populate our celebrity-crazy culture.

No doubt this desire to be in the know comes from our natural drive for knowledge motivated by our curiosity. Also at work is the feeling of being special and powerful when we are in possession of knowledge that others lack and/or wish to know. We become sought out. Our opinions are listened to. Others care what we think and say. Unfortunately much of what passes for knowledge is really trivial and just gossip.

There is a deeper knowledge that we need if we are to be happy and know peace. Such knowledge is not obtained from a tabloid but comes from opening our hearts to the revealed word of God. And this knowledge concerns the very nature of God as the eternal, all-powerful Creator of heaven and earth. In the midst of our trials and struggles, the Lord is there to support us when we are weary, strengthen us when we are about to faint, and revive our hearts when we lose hope.

The season of Advent reminds us that the eternal Wisdom of God becomes visible in the child Jesus. The Lord renews our strength and helps us to soar as with eagles' wings. The knowledge God offers us is the very foundation of all wisdom and truth. Namely, God loves us unconditionally. Have you not heard? Listen with your heart so you may be wise in the Lord.

Reflection Questions. The Lord is the very essence of holiness. God is holy and expects His people to be holy as well. Those who trust in the Lord will have their strength renewed and not be abandoned.

How have I grown in holiness during this Advent season?

_____
_____
_____
_____
_____

In what ways have I grown weary and faint in the spiritual life?

_____
_____
_____
_____
_____

How has the Lord renewed my strength for the life of faith?

_____
_____
_____
_____
_____

Jesus comes into our human condition to provide rest and comfort. Jesus especially seeks out those who are burdened by the trials of everyday life. The humble heart of Jesus offers comfort to the poor and wretched of the earth.

What are the daily concerns of life that weary my spirit?

_____
_____
_____
_____

What material needs have caused me to worry about the future?

How have I helped to share the burden of others by Christian love?

Closing Conversation. Spend a few minutes prayerfully reading the Gospel. Write your responses to Jesus.

Jesus: Are you afraid to come to me with your burdens and trials? Why?

Response:

Jesus: How have you become more gentle and humble with others?

Response:

Jesus: What spiritual strength have you drawn from my gentle and humble heart?

Response:

Thursday OF THE SECOND WEEK

Isaiah 41:13-20 It is the Lord alone who has saved Israel in all her trials. To trust in military power, material abundance, or political alliance is foolish. Yahweh saves His people and in Him alone is the nation to rejoice.

Matthew 11:11-15 The role of the prophet is to speak the word of God. The prophet often becomes the object of hostility and violence. John the Baptizer comes as the herald of the Messiah. He, too, will be put to death. Yet the words of Jesus remind us that "history has not known a man born of woman greater than John the Baptizer."

A Man Called John

There is a cost to discipleship. And at times the cost may be the very laying down of our lives in imitation of Jesus. The Hebrew Scriptures are filled with the stories of the men and women of faith who made the ultimate sacrifice in order to remain faithful to the Lord. These heroes and heroines of faith made the decision to obey God rather than men. They made the decision to walk in the valley of darkness knowing that the Light of Life would lead them to restful waters.

John the Baptizer is the herald of Jesus as the Lamb of God who takes away our sins. The vocation of John to be herald comes at a dear price. John is not excused from the demands of following the Lord. Even less is he spared the hatred and opposition that come to those who proclaim a Lord superior to all earthly lords and principalities. The response of the world to the Kingdom and the preaching of the Gospel is violence and opposition. Jesus tells the crowds: "From John the Baptizer's time until now the Kingdom of God has suffered violence, and the violent take it by force." Violence against the Kingdom of God and those who witness to the Gospel, continues in our own day. Throughout the world — Latin America, Eastern Europe, South Africa — we witness the violence of the world against those who work for peace, justice, and freedom in the name of the Prince of Peace.

Most of us do not face dramatic challenges to our faith. However, our challenges are no less real or important. For us it is the daily commitment to Jesus and the Kingdom. We suffer violence from a culture which is often indifferent to Gospel values. We suffer rejection for our beliefs from social groups. We may even be denied a job or a promotion because we believe in Jesus. In our own quiet and unnoticed way, let us follow the example of a man named John and remain faithful to God's Kingdom of Peace.

Reflection Questions. In the midst of Israel's fear and despair the word of the Lord comes through Isaiah: "Fear not, I will help you." The God of the mighty deeds of Exodus is also the God who will once again free His people. In the fullness of time, Jesus will come to replace all fear with love.

Have I respected nature as part of God's good creation? How?

_____
_____
_____
_____

How does the wonder and beauty of nature speak to me of God's creative love?

_____
_____
_____
_____

Have I been generous with my resources, especially toward the poor and needy?

_____
_____
_____
_____
_____

Jesus tells us of the greatness of John the Baptizer because of his role in salvation history. Yet through our baptism into Christ, we are greater than he. That is, we are called to witness to the death and resurrection of Jesus.

What quality do I most admire in John the Baptizer? Why?

_____
_____
_____
_____

Who are some of our modern-day prophets calling us to conversion?

Why does the Kingdom of God suffer violence?

Closing Conversation. Prayerfully read the Gospel. Write your answers in response to Jesus.

Jesus: Can you accept the preaching of the Gospel? Are you fearful?

Response:

Jesus: How have you suffered for the Kingdom?

Response:

Jesus: How have you helped your parish become a prophetic witness to the Kingdom?

Response:

Friday OF THE SECOND WEEK

Isaiah 48:17-19   The Lord of Israel is their redeemer. No other nation has known the will of the Lord. It is only to Israel that the Lord has revealed the commandments. The Lord's commandments are good, and all who obey them will gain life everlasting.

Matthew 11:16-19   Jesus tells the crowd that more is required than mere words and having a good time if one is to be a disciple. To follow Jesus means to suffer opposition and lies. Only those with a strong faith will persevere to the end.

He is mad!

Sometimes no matter what you do you cannot be successful or please others. In our Gospel reading Jesus comes to just such a conclusion. Many in the crowd rejected John because they found him too rigid and demanding. John called for change and a conversion of heart. Many were willing to follow John so long as it didn't cost too much or require too much of a change in values and lifestyle.

With Jesus the complaint is just the opposite. Jesus is not serious enough or He associates with all the wrong people, namely, tax collectors and those outside the law. No doubt the same ones who were rejecting John as too austere are rejecting Jesus because He is too lax. Again, sometimes no matter what you do you cannot win.

However, neither Jesus nor John the Baptizer were concerned with being successful or winning approval. Both men wanted to be faithful to the mission given them by God. Jesus goes on to say that true wisdom will be found by those who remain faithful to their call no matter what others think. Our ultimate destiny will be determined by the content of our hearts and the way in which we have remained faithful to the person of Jesus.

The Christian will always appear to the world to be mad. The values and judgments of the world are not ours. We proclaim a different Lord than the false gods of money, power, popularity, and sexual pleasure. We dare to proclaim a Lord who comes into our human condition. We witness to a God who takes on flesh. We live in the hope of the Child who comes announcing peace. Indeed we are mad!

Reflection Questions. The covenant with Abraham is once again remembered and renewed: "Your descendants would be like the sand... Their name never cut off or blotted out from my presence." Even in the most trying of times the Lord is at work redeeming His people.

Do I obediently accept the commands of God? Explain.

_____
_____
_____
_____

What recent experience has taught me to follow the Lord's commands?

_____
_____
_____

Who has been a source of spiritual strength in helping me follow the Lord? How?

_____
_____
_____

Some people can only follow Jesus if they can be guaranteed a good time or a life free from pain. This, however, is not the way to follow Jesus. Those who become disciples of Jesus will often experience rejection.

Do I have difficulty accepting the austere dimensions of the Gospel? Explain.

_____
_____
_____

What is my reaction to Jesus associating with tax collectors and those outside the law?

_____
_____
_____

42 MY ADVENT JOURNAL

At times do I find the teachings of Jesus unrealistic or even mad?

___

Closing Conversation. Spend a few minutes in quiet prayer. Think about the reaction of the crowds to John and Jesus. Write your responses to the following.

Jesus: Do you find the preaching of John too demanding?

Response: ___

Jesus: Are you able to relate to the joyful and austere aspects of the Gospel? How?

Response: ___

Jesus: Are you able to relate to the outsider and those who are rejected?

Response: ___

Saturday OF THE SECOND WEEK

Sirach 48:1-4, 9-11 Elijah is considered the greatest of the Hebrew prophets and the most mysterious of God's messengers. Tradition held that he would reappear to usher in the Messianic age. The day of the Lord will come not with fire but with the birth of the child Jesus.

Matthew 17:10-13 Just as in the Hebrew Scriptures, Elijah must come before the Day of the Lord, John the Baptizer came to announce Jesus as the Messiah. However, the leaders rejected John and put him to death. The same fate awaits the Son of Man.

Suffer at their hands

It seems strange, and downright out of place, to speak of suffering during the season of Advent. This is supposed to be the time of peace and healing. Talk of suffering seems to belong to Lent and not the season to be jolly. However, it is just because this is the time of God's unbounded love that suffering is most appropriate. The coming of the Word into our flesh gives visible expression to God's great love. And the good news of God's love proves to be bad news for the self-righteous and those religious leaders who want human praise more than the glory of God.

Jesus does not try to minimize the cost of the Incarnation. St. Paul, writing to the Philippians (2:6), tells them that Christ emptied Himself of divinity and glory so as to take on our human condition. Furthermore, in becoming human, Jesus took the form of a slave and suffered our very human death as He also partook in our very human birth. Jesus is not spared the pain of the human condition. In fact, He suffered a great deal at the hands of those who could make no room in their hearts for Him in the poor, the sinful and the outcast. Jesus, as the Son of Man, comes to announce a time of grace to a world burdened by sin and death. Unfortunately many still look for deliverance from the principalities and powers of this world.

Advent is the season when our thoughts turn to the child Jesus. It is also a time when we look through the crib to see the Son of Man who "will suffer at the hands" of the mighty and religiously smug. To love much is to know suffering. To love much is also to experience the mystery of God and His love for us.

Reflection Questions. The book of Sirach recounts the wisdom and faith of God's chosen people. One such hero is Elijah. The Israelites expected him to return so as to usher in the Day of the Lord.

Does the Second Coming of the Lord fill me with fear? Hope? Explain.

_____
_____
_____
_____

How have I experienced God's absence in my life recently?

_____
_____
_____
_____

In what ways have I practiced a zealous faith like that of the prophet Elijah?

_____
_____
_____
_____

The title "Son of Man" is the most frequent one ascribed to Jesus in the New Testament. This mysterious figure is not only associated with judgment at the end of the world but also with the Suffering Servant of the Lord. The Son of Man must suffer and be rejected before He enters into His glory.

How have I failed to help others come to know Jesus?

_____
_____
_____
_____

SATURDAY OF THE SECOND WEEK

During the past year how have I failed to recognize Jesus in my daily life?

In what ways have I helped others to know Jesus and experience Him in their daily life?

Closing Conversation. Spend quiet moments in prayer. Reflect on the question of Jesus. Write your response.

Jesus: If I were to return today, what about your life would you want to change?

Response:

III. PAUL: THE MYSTERY OF GOD'S LOVE

*P*aul is the man for all seasons. His life captures the many shades of God's love at work shining through our human weakness. Our first encounter with Paul is as Saul: the one zealous for the ways of the Hebrew covenant. His dedication was so great that we see him as a leader in the killing of the martyr Stephen (Ac 7:54-60). Yet we know that God is able to write straight with the crooked lines of our lives. God's grace is able to take our strengths and use them for the sake of the Kingdom. So Saul will become Paul, the apostle to the Gentiles. The zealot for the Hebrew law will become the ambassador for Christ and tell of the infinite richness of grace poured into our hearts.

The life of Paul reminds us of a deep truth about the meaning of the Christian story and the wonder of this season: we can always begin again. The boundless, free gift of grace took root in Paul's life and changed him at the very core of his being. This man who had it all together experienced a shaking of the foundations and a new direction to his life. The change was so profound that he was able to write to the Christians at Philippi: "But those things I used to consider gain I have now reappraised as loss in light of Christ. I have come to rate all as loss in the light of the surpassing knowledge of my Lord Jesus Christ" (Ph 3:7-8).

Regardless of our personal situation we all at times feel the need to change and draw closer to Christ. We feel that we have traveled far from our Father's house and away from our loved ones. We feel the pain of guilt over past sins. Our lives have fallen short of God's glory and we are weighted down with feelings of self-hatred and inadequacy. God's grace transforming the life of Paul can do the same for us. On our own personal "roads to Damascus" the Lord waits to encounter us. Advent is the season when the mystery of God's love becomes visible. That holy love took on flesh in the child Jesus and then transformed Saul into Paul. That holy love awaits our hearts to open so we, too, may be born anew.

Sunday OF THE THIRD WEEK

Rejoice always

The exhortation to "rejoice always" comes to us through the first letter of Paul to the Thessalonians (1 Th 5:16). No doubt we feel that such an invitation is unnecessary. Advent and Christmas raise our spirits. We have little trouble reaching spiritual highs and warm feelings toward God and our neighbor. After all, during Advent we await the coming of the Word made flesh. And while we are waiting for Christmas it would seem that the exhortation to rejoice is not needed.

However, Paul knows there is a profound difference between rejoicing in the Holy Spirit and the joy offered by the world. Much of what we call joy is just superficial good feelings brought on by getting what we want. In time these feelings pass and we become bored and begin looking for a new object to please us. We spend so much of our life looking for that one person, place or thing which will still our restless heart and fill us with a joy no one can take away.

Paul believed he had found joy and peace in the law. Yet Paul came to see that the law and the externals of religion could not provide real joy. In fact, the law filled him with anxiety and feelings of wretchedness. The law was powerless to give lasting joy to the spirit. Only Jesus the Christ could fill Paul's heart with a joy that would remain through the many trials of his adventure of faith. Joy in the Holy Spirit is not a passing feeling but an abiding presence. Joy in the Holy Spirit is ever present through all the changing circumstances of our lives.

During Advent, and especially as we move toward Christmas, the talk of joy fills the air. Unfortunately the true joy of the Spirit may not fill our hearts. We can easily be distracted and settle for a fleeting pleasure rather than the joy which rang out on that first Christmas: "Glory to God in high heaven, peace on earth to those on whom his favor rests" (Lk 2:14). These words are not frozen in time but come to us now. God is about to do a new thing. Do you not see it? Does not your heart quicken with joy?

SUNDAY OF THE THIRD WEEK

Closing Conversation. Read St. Paul's letter to the Romans 14:17-19. Prayerfully write your response to St. Paul.

St. Paul: In what ways have you been an instrument of God's Kingdom of joy? How have you helped the sorrowful to find joy in the Holy Spirit?

Response:

St. Paul: How has your faith become more than a series of intellectual propositions and moral rules? Has your relationship with Jesus matured? Explain.

Response:

Monday OF THE THIRD WEEK

Numbers 24:2-7, 15-17 Balaam is a prophet filled with the spirit of the Lord. He hears the word of God and reports it faithfully. Israel will prevail over its enemies through the providence of God.

Matthew 21:23-27 Jesus confronts the religious leaders over the issue of authority. The chief priests and elders want to know what is the moral foundation for Jesus' teachings. However, Jesus refuses to answer because he knows they just want to trap Him.

On what authority?

Humankind has always struggled with the issue of authority. In the Garden of Eden, Adam and Eve gave in to the serpent's temptation to reject God's authority. We know the sorry consequences which followed. In our own day we witness a general suspicion and rejection of all authority. Traditional roles such as parent, teacher, clergy, politician and businessman no longer command respect. In fact, some see these roles as outdated and even dangerous to the well–being of society. Furthermore, large institutions no longer carry the authority to influence daily life and public opinion they once did. Religion, school, family, government, and medicine are often viewed as doing great harm to the individual. While not denying abuses are present in our institutions, it is very dangerous to reject all social roles and institutions. In the absence of tradition, social roles and institutional life, we are forced back on the puny resources of the individual self. This is dangerous because we can be easily manipulated by the mass media, the commercial power of Madison Avenue and the cultural influences of powerful charismatic figures. Without authority we can easily be tossed about by every whim and cultural mood.

The question put to Jesus is crucial: "On what authority are you doing these things?" Jesus' authority rests on His fidelity to the will of the Father. Jesus came into the world, and our human condition, so that we might know the will of God and love with enduring love. Jesus does not come to judge and condemn but to save. He does not come to proclaim Himself but to make visible the Father's compassion for all His children. The authority of Jesus is not one which seeks His own glory but the glory of the Father.

The authority of all who rule and govern must always be grounded in the will of God. No earthly authority has power in and of itself. Everything belongs to the Lord and we are called to be good stewards of His many gifts. Those in authority are to seek the common good and show special care for the weak and powerless. This is exactly what Jesus does for each of us. He shows us special care in our need.

Reflection Questions. Entering the Promised Land is one thing; remaining is another. The enemies of Israel surround her. Once again, as in the time of the Exodus, Israel must trust in the Lord if she is to be vindicated.

In what ways have I tried to turn my enemies into friends?

In what ways has the Lord protected me from evil?

Do I find it difficult to pray for those who persecute me? Explain.

The chief priests and elders confront Jesus about His teaching because they are concerned about their power more than truth or God's glory. They reject Jesus in the same way they rejected John the Baptizer. Jesus' authority comes from who He is and His relationship with the Father in the Spirit.

Do I easily rebel against authority? Why?

Do I prayerfully and respectfully listen to the teaching of those in religious authority?

In exercising authority, do I respect others and seek the glory of God?

Closing Conversation. Spend a few minutes in quiet reflection on the Gospel. Write your response to Jesus' question.

Jesus: On what authority or foundation does your faith rest? Explain.

Response:

Tuesday OF THE THIRD WEEK

Zephaniah 3:1-2, 9-13 The Lord is always faithful to His promises. Unfortunately, Israel does not always remember the covenant. National arrogance frequently comes into play as Israel seeks security in worshiping false gods and forming military alliances. Yet the only refuge is in the name of the Lord.

Matthew 21:28-32 Jesus requires more than words. Faith must always be put into action. The most unlikely response to Jesus comes from the tax collectors and prostitutes. Unfortunately, it is those who claim to be obedient to God who reject Jesus and the Gospel.

I will leave a remnant

The temptation is always great for us to cut our losses and get out of a bad situation. These days it's considered good sense to get out of dead-end relationships and contracts which do not maximize profits. There is very little support in the general culture for keeping one's word and following through on one's commitments. If the going gets tough just get going. Forget the consequences of such a lifestyle. What is crucial, supposedly, is that one keeps one's options open. It is imperative to have an option.

The Lord does not deal with us that way. In the time of Zephaniah, the people have gone astray. Israel "hears no voice, accepts no correction." She no longer puts her trust in the Lord who formed her long ago and brought her out of Egypt. Yet the Lord will not destroy His people or cancel the covenant. Instead He will "leave as a remnant in your midst a people humble and lowly." This remnant of Israel will trust in the Lord and serve as a reminder of where truth and peace are to be found.

The Christian community continues to be a remnant in the world. The community of faith is not to be of the world but is to remain in the world as a witness to the true Lord of history, creation, and the human heart. The world will always seek to erect its own idols for destruction and its own golden calves to worship. Hence, the Christian community must be ever present and faithful to the good news of the Word made flesh. In so doing the world can have the real hope of redemption through the loving sacrifice of the One who is to be born in our midst.

Reflection Questions. Jerusalem, the holy city, has turned away from the Lord and become "rebellious and polluted." The disobedience of the people means they no longer hear the word of Yahweh or seek to do His will. However, God will remain faithful by raising up a remnant to continue the covenant.

Does my city seek justice and work for the common good?

_____
_____
_____
_____

Does my city take special care of the homeless and poor?

_____
_____
_____
_____

Do the city leaders give good example of civic pride and virtue?

_____
_____
_____
_____

Jesus comes to announce the good news of salvation. The ultimate victory does not belong to sin and death but to grace and new life. The sinners and rejected flock to Jesus because He gives them cause to hope.

How have I applied my belief in Jesus to my daily life during Advent?

_____
_____
_____
_____

TUESDAY OF THE THIRD WEEK

Do I experience difficulty in putting my moral values into practice? How?

In what ways have I turned from sin and experienced Christian freedom and joy?

Closing Conversation. Prayerfully reflect on the Gospel selection. Meditate on Jesus' question. Write your response.

Jesus: Do you have trouble experiencing my grace and acceptance? Why? What is preventing you from believing in my love? How can I help you in your journey of faith?

Response:

Wednesday OF THE THIRD WEEK

Isaiah 45:6-8, 18, 21-25   The lowest point in Israel's history took place in 587 B.C. with the destruction of the temple at Jerusalem and the subsequent exile to Babylon. It was the result of Israel's infidelity to the covenant. Vindication will take place, however, because of the Lord's love and fidelity.

Luke 7:18-23   Jesus is asked if He is the Messiah or is there another to come. He does not answer John's disciples directly. Rather, He tells them to report back to John what they hear and see: the cripples walk, the blind see, and the poor have the good news preached to them.

Let justice also spring up

During this season the air is filled with talk of peace and reconciliation. The warmth of the season draws us closer to one another and even moves us to act on behalf of those in need. We hear a great deal about charity and sharing. What is often missing is the necessary talk about justice, for peace and reconciliation are only possible if we first seek justice.

Our image of justice is quite different from the biblical experience of it. We understand justice symbolized by Lady Justice. She is blindfolded and holding a set of equally balanced scales. Our view of justice is one which emphasizes impartiality and equality. Of course these are important aspects of justice. After all, much injustice is done because equals are treated unequally and the powerful take care of their own.

The Bible approaches justice from a different perspective. Justice is generosity. Biblical justice seeks out those most in need and responds in abundant measure. Biblical justice does not look for merit but looks toward the powerless and those without resources. Jesus is the very justice of God because He seeks out the powerless, the sinful, and the wretched so as to affirm their dignity and He announces that the good news is especially for them. And it is for them not because they deserve the gift but because they need to hear they are accepted and loved.

Advent and Christmas are the acceptable times to let justice spring up in our hearts, homes and world. Justice is not some dry, impartial set of rules. It is the generous gift of God's limitless love for us. The justice we have received we are to give to others. To be about the work of justice, which is generosity, is to know the true peace and reconciliation of this holy season.

Reflection Questions. The Lord of history is also the Divine Artist who created the earth to be used wisely and justly. We do not own the resources of creation. Rather, we are to be good stewards of the Lord's gifts. God's good creation is destined to be part of the new creation of Jesus.

How have I experienced the generosity of God during Advent?

_____
_____
_____
_____

How have I worked to enhance the earth and be a good steward of God's creation?

_____
_____
_____
_____

In what ways has the Lord's generosity helped me to endure my trials?

_____
_____
_____
_____

The people were long suffering. They were desperately seeking a Messiah. Many thought it might be John. John, though, clearly indicated he was not the Promised One. The disciples of John came to Jesus to find out if He were the Messiah. Jesus does not answer with words but with deeds: deeds of compassion toward those in need.

Have I reached out to the sick and those confined to hospitals during Advent?

_____
_____
_____
_____
_____

58 MY ADVENT JOURNAL

In what ways have I been searching for the Messiah during Advent?

_____
_____
_____
_____

What corporal works of mercy have I practiced during Advent?

_____
_____
_____
_____

Closing Conversation. After spending a few minutes in quiet reflection, write your responses to Jesus.

Jesus: What is your reaction to my ministry of healing?

Response: _____
_____
_____
_____
_____

Jesus: Do you find me a stumbling block?

Response: _____
_____
_____
_____
_____
_____

Thursday OF THE THIRD WEEK

Isaiah 54:1-10 This selection from Isaiah is one of the most beautiful in all of Scripture. The Lord is hesed, that is, faithful, enduring love for His people. The anger of the Lord will not last forever. The tender and powerful love of God abides.

Luke 7:24-30 Looks can be deceiving. John did not look the part of a great prophet or mighty religious leader. John was the final messenger sent by God to prepare hearts for the Word made flesh. The proud and self-righteous could not accept John or Jesus.

Enduring love

One of our most familiar phrases is "falling in love." What does this phrase say about how we experience and understand love? To connect love with falling denotes something accidental, misguided, and even painful. Love, we are told is blind and the Cupid child is the symbol of this blind emotion. Cupid shoots the arrow and no one knows where it will land. Such views of love are divorced of intention, purpose, direction, and a sense of desiring the good of the beloved. One can fall in and out of love. Cupid can pierce us today and next week miss the heart. Love is unpredictable and risky business.

The Bible does not hold up to us the Cupid child along with the Christ child as the living sign of God's enduring love for us. God's love is anything but accidental, misguided or fickle. God's love is hesed, that is, enduring forever. It transcends all time and circumstance. God does not fall in and out of love with us. He is always in love with us. Our reading from Isaiah puts it so beautifully: "With enduring love, I take pity on you... My love shall never leave you nor my covenant of peace be shaken, says the Lord who has mercy on you." This is not a blind love. It is not a love which results from a fickle heart or a passing emotion. God's love is for us forever.

If ever we find ourselves doubting God's faithful love, all we need do is draw near the crib in Bethlehem. God becoming human flesh says that He is committed to us forever. God will never turn away from us or fall out of love with us. His love is not accidental. Our hearts are not preparing for Cupid but for Jesus. God looks into our hearts and drives out all fear with enduring love. And such a love is no accident.

Reflection Questions. When the Lord forgives, He forgets. The imagery of marriage is used by the prophet to express the Lord's forgiveness of Israel. A good marriage requires a faithful love, a love that is willing to forget past hurts.

How has my marriage (or, if single, some friendship) brought me closer to the Lord?

___

Do I have trouble forgetting past hurts even though I offer forgiveness? What recent experience with a spouse or friend has taught me the grace of forgetting and forgiving?

___

The grace of God continues to surprise. The wretched and the marginal members of society find comfort in the preaching and healing ministries of Jesus. Unfortunately, the learned and the clever often close their hearts to Him.

Do I judge others by their external appearance rather than by their actions?

___

Have I made an effort to respect the values of others? How?

___

THURSDAY OF THE THIRD WEEK 61

In what ways have I made the stranger welcome in my community, parish, school, home or place of business?

Closing Conversation. Spend a few moments in prayerful reflection on the Gospel. Write your response to Jesus.

Jesus: How have you reaffirmed your baptismal commitments during Advent?

Response:

Jesus: How have you provided the young with a good Christian example?

Response:

Jesus: How have you helped to support your religious leaders in their ministry?

Response:

Friday OF THE THIRD WEEK

Isaiah 56:1-3, 6-8   There is a deep sense of urgency in this selection from Isaiah. The people must reform their lives by doing what is just and right. All who do the will of the Lord will be gathered by Yahweh.

John 5:33-36   The Gospel of John presents us with two kinds or degrees of faith: imperfect and perfect. Imperfect faith is one which accepts Jesus because of His works. If we don't accept Jesus because of His teachings then the mighty works He does indicate the Father sent Him.

Loving the name of the Lord

What's in a name? We moderns are tempted to say, "Nothing." After all, we have it on good authority that names are just words which point to persons or things. Names are social conventions which can easily change. A rose by any other name would smell as sweet. Hence, the idea that there is something in a name strikes us as strange.

From the perspective of the Bible, there is a great deal in a name. To know the name of someone or to name a thing is to have intimate knowledge and some control over that person or thing. A name reveals the person and makes known a key aspect of his or her being or character. Adam named the animals in the garden and in so doing tells us something about their nature. In the New Testament Simon becomes Peter, and Saul will be called Paul. Yahweh does not tell His name to Moses on Sinai. Rather, He indicates that He is to be called "I am who I am." The people are not to have control over Yahweh. It is He who is in control of their destiny and not the other way around. It is Yahweh who will give them a name and a land so they may prosper and know the Lord.

Jesus comes into our world to reveal the name of the Father. And the name of God is LOVE. The God who is I AM is faithful love. The crib and the cross speak to us of God's name: love. God loves us so much He becomes like us in Jesus. God's love is so powerful that He is able to overcome our chief enemies, sin and death. And He does so on the cross. To love the name of the Lord is to respond to Love itself. This Divine Love is at the very center of the universe moving all things to their proper end. This Divine Love desires to take root in our hearts so that we may be reborn. And in the words of Isaiah: "Thus says the Lord, ... 'My salvation is about to come'."

Reflection Questions. To do the will of God is to experience genuine happiness. The commandments are not meant to be heavy burdens but a set of sure guides which help us to love the Lord and our neighbor. In time all people will come to know the Lord and His way of peace.

Which commandment of the Lord presents the greatest spiritual challenge to me?

_____

_____

_____

_____

How have I confronted this challenge (prayer, fasting, or the like)?

_____

_____

_____

_____

Have I been able to see God's call to spiritual maturity behind the commandments? How?

_____

_____

_____

_____

The ministry of John the Baptizer has come and gone. Jesus is present among the people. The true Light has come into the world. It is time for all who hear the preaching of Jesus and witness His works to believe that He is indeed the Son of God.

Have I been a Christian, a light-bearer, in my home, school or work place?

_____

_____

_____

_____

MY ADVENT JOURNAL

Have I experienced opposition? How? Why?

___

How have I shared in the works of Jesus in my daily life?

___

Closing Conversation. Spend a few minutes in quiet reflection. Write your response to Jesus.

Jesus: I have come to do the work of my Father in heaven. Next to each of the works of my Father indicate how you have carried on these works of love.

Prayer: ___

Fellowship with outcasts: ___

Visiting the sick and imprisoned: ___

IV. MARY: THE MOTHERLY LOVE OF GOD

No discussion of Advent would be complete without turning our attention to Mary. Unfortunately the role and the meaning of Mary has been greatly misunderstood in recent years. Some believe that the Catholic-Christian story would be better told if we downplayed Mary or ignored her altogether. The usual abuses are listed: the danger that in honoring Mary we overlook the grace of God; some raised Mary to an almost goddess status; and a great deal of abuses have arisen over popular piety concerning devotion to the Blessed Mother.

Others believe that the ultimate hope for the Church and the world rest on a revival of Marian devotions. These Christians believe that many of the abuses in the Church and moral failures in the world result from a lack of devotion to Mary as the Mother of God. Both of these positions contain important truths up to a point. However, both positions need one another if we are to better appreciate Mary and what her life means for us and tells us about God.

Mary is such a crucial Advent figure not only because of her obvious role as the Mother of Jesus, but also because Mary is the symbol of God's motherly love for us. God loves us like a mother. To gaze on the crib and see Mary with the child Jesus is to be reminded of the ways in which God loves us. Our God loves us with a love that is nurturing, life-giving, tender, protective, unconditional, non-judgmental, and absolute. Mary reminds us that we can always approach God regardless of our past. God's love always makes possible a new day and a new life.

To celebrate Mary is to celebrate God's grace shining through our human condition. When we look to Mary, we see one like us; hence she offers us hope. When we look to Mary with the child Jesus, we see God's motherly love for us. Pray we have the living faith to accept such a hope and love.

Sunday OF THE FOURTH WEEK

Blessed are you among women

When the angel Gabriel first appeared to Mary she felt anything but blessed or highly favored. St. Luke tells us that Mary was "deeply troubled by his words" and had no idea what they meant (Lk 1:26-38). This is a very natural and human reaction to divine revelation. In the presence of the Lord we are filled with awe. We are overcome with a deep sense of being unworthy. The Lord is holiness itself and we have fallen short of God's glory. In the Hebrew Scriptures we read that the prophet Isaiah felt he was perishing when confronted by the Lord (chapter 6). Mary, one like us in her total humanity, is now being called to play a vital role in salvation history.

The angel goes on to tell Mary she is not to give in to fear. Rather, she is to experience God's favor through the birth of Jesus. This, however, only adds to her anxiety. Mary is a virgin and conception is not possible. The angel assures Mary that she will conceive not in the natural way, but in a supernatural way through the power of the Holy Spirit. Mary's child will be the Messiah.

No doubt the angel's words did not make everything clear and distinct. In fact, his words may have only added to her anxiety and confusion. Nevertheless, Mary accepted the Lord's message in complete trust. Mary knew that faith does not always mean complete understanding. Mary knew that doubt often accompanies faith. Faith is always being tested by the experiences of life. These experiences need not be dramatic such as the death of a loved one or a revelation from heaven. Our faith can be tested in the daily struggles we face at home, work or school: the challenge to love those who hurt us; the challenge to be honest and exhibit a sense of personal integrity; and the ability to forgive those who have hurt us deeply, can all test our faith. The meaning of these challenges may not be clear immediately; the meaning of some will never be known to us.

What is crucial is that we follow the example of Mary and surrender in complete trust to the Lord.

Advent is the season of God's abundant blessings. We may not always feel blessed. Our hearts know anxiety and fear. Yet the words of the angel to Mary are for us as well: "Do not fear." Let us pray that we can make the words of Mary our own: "I am the servant of the Lord. Let it be done to me as you say." All of our concerns will not disappear. However, we will be able to go forward with the confident assurance that we are blessed in the Holy Spirit.

SUNDAY OF THE FOURTH WEEK

Closing Conversation. Spend a few minutes in quiet prayer. Reflect on the life of Mary and her life of faith. Write your responses to Mary.

Mary: Tell me of a recent spiritual challenge which caused you some anxiety.

Response: _____

_____

_____

_____

Mary: How did you respond to this spiritual challenge?

Response: _____

_____

_____

_____

Mary: In what ways have you been a servant of the Lord in your daily life?

Response: _____

_____

_____

_____

Mary: How has the Lord brought new life out of what seemed a hopeless situation?

Response: _____

_____

_____

_____

Novena DECEMBER 17

Genesis 49:2, 8-10 The great patriarch of Israel, Jacob, calls his sons together for a final blessing and some words of wisdom. If they continue to lead the people in the ways of the covenant all will go well. If they forget the Lord then tragedy will follow.

Matthew 1:1-17 Matthew records the ancestry of Jesus in order to show He is the Messiah. With the birth of Jesus the promises of Yahweh are fulfilled. The Kingdom of God is about to be established in a definitive way with the birth of Jesus.

The family record of Jesus

One of our deepest childhood fears is the fear of being adopted. At one time or another we wonder if our parents are really our parents. We ask them for reassurance. We have this need to know our roots. We want to make sure we belong. We want to make sure we are part of the right family story. Our identity is social. And essential to who we are is the realization of the common story we share with previous generations.

The Gospel of Matthew contains the genealogy of Jesus. At first blush this can seem to be nothing more than a long list of impossible names to pronounce. However, on closer inspection we see that this genealogy tells us something very important about salvation history. Namely, the promise of salvation made to our father in faith, Abraham, has been fulfilled with the birth of Jesus. The Lord is faithful to His promises. The time of deliverance is near. God is now about to do a new thing. A new stage in revelation is about to dawn. The Word of the Lord will now be present in our midst in the person of Jesus.

Each of us through Baptism has been grafted into the family tree of Jesus Christ. The succeeding generations have told the story of the child Jesus and the One who is risen from the dead. Each Christian continues to live the story of God among us in the Word made flesh. During this season of Advent we must remember our roots. We are connected with the child in the crib and that one great story of faith which extends to the very beginning of humankind.

Reflection Questions. Those in authority must be more aware of their responsibility and then their power. The leaders of the community of faith must guide the people so as to be faithful to the covenant. Only then will God's blessing protect the community and peace abide.

How have I grown in faith through the example of the saints and biblical figures?

How have the traditions of my faith helped me to grow close to Jesus?

Do I feel that religious traditions hinder my spiritual growth? Explain.

We are members of God's family through the Incarnation and the Paschal Mystery. This membership calls for us to remember our dignity as followers of Christ. Membership in God's family comes at a cost. We must be willing to be born anew and daily carry our cross.

How do I witness to being a living member of God's family?

Have I worked for greater understanding between Christians and Jews? How?

How have I worked to bring the stranger and the foreigner into the Christian community?

Closing Conversation. Spend a few minutes in quiet prayer. Write your response to Jesus about family life.

Jesus: What is the most pressing need of your family? How can I help?

Response: _____

Jesus: How has being a member of the Christian family strengthened your home life?

Response: _____

Novena DECEMBER 18

Jeremiah 23:5-8 Yahweh is the Lord of history and reveals His holy will through the covenant with Israel. During the time of Jeremiah, Israel is ruled by a king. The prophet speaks of a time of restoration and deliverance. Justice and peace will be established through David's dynasty.

Matthew 1:18-24 The central figure of Jesus' birth in the Gospel of Matthew is Joseph. He is a man of integrity who desires to do the will of God. Joseph, like Mary, is open to receive a message from the Lord. He takes Mary as his wife who will give birth to Jesus.

The Lord our justice

In recent times we have witnessed a number of political scandals. Our political leaders, those entrusted with the common good, have broken faith with those they are to serve. Such scandals weaken social bonds of trust and give rise to a general atmosphere of cynicism. Worst of all, citizens begin to feel that they must be dishonest if they are to survive. The moral well-being of the community suffers as each person begins to seek his or her own private advantage at the expense of the common good. Interest groups flourish which put pressure on political leaders to serve only their narrow concerns and not the good of the whole community. In time community life ceases to exist. Each person is left on his or her own to get what they can by whatever means no matter who is hurt.

There is, of course, nothing new about political scandals. Power always runs the risk of being corrupted; and of being absolutely corrupted when left unaccountable. The Hebrew Scriptures are filled with examples of political leaders who became arrogant and thought they were above the covenant. Such leaders came to believe that they could do as they pleased and ignore the will of God. The folly of this position is revealed in one disaster after another, for when the ways of the Lord are forgotten, the people suffer both materially and spiritually. For example, even the great King David sinned and brought disaster on the nation.

During Advent, we await the coming of the Prince of Peace and the King of Kings. We need to remember that this peace is God's gift based on justice and respect for the individual person. The Kingship of Jesus is one which recognizes the absolute authority of the Father. As Christians we have a responsibility to pray for our earthly leaders, promote the common good, and help to establish a peace grounded in God's justice.

72 MY ADVENT JOURNAL

Reflection Questions. Messianism is an important part of the religious life of Israel. The king is not just a political figure but one who receives an anointing from the Lord in the spirit. The king is entrusted with the covenant. The prophet Jeremiah speaks of that time when David's dynasty will be restored.

What is my attitude toward political leaders? Have I prayed for my civic leaders?

_____
_____
_____
_____

In what ways does my faith influence my political values and activities?

_____
_____
_____
_____

In what ways has our world made progress in receiving the peace of Christ?

_____
_____
_____
_____

The prophet Jeremiah spoke of the time when God would establish the Messianic age of salvation. The birth of Jesus establishes in a unique way the presence of God with His people. Joseph listens to the angel and takes Mary as his wife.

During this Advent have I been open to God's special word to me?

_____
_____
_____
_____

DECEMBER 18   73

Have I recently had a mystical experience? Explain.

_____
_____
_____
_____

Have I been a person of integrity in my relationship with God and neighbor? Explain.

_____
_____
_____
_____

Closing Conversation.   Spend a few minutes in prayer. Reflect on the statements of Joseph. Write your responses.

Joseph: Have you had to keep a commitment that challenged your faith? Explain.

Response: _____
_____
_____
_____

Joseph: Has God asked you to do a work which seemed beyond your ability? Explain.

Response: _____
_____
_____
_____

Joseph: Do you feel resentful when your work goes unnoticed? Explain.

Response: _____
_____
_____
_____

Novena DECEMBER 19

Judges 13:2-7, 24-25 This selection recounts the birth of Samson. The spirit of the Lord was with him from the beginning. Samson will be consecrated to the Lord and deliver Israel from the Philistines. Jesus will come and deliver all peoples from sin and death.

Luke 1:5-25 John the Baptizer reminds us of the special births of Samuel and Samson. From the moment of conception John is chosen to do a special work for the Lord. John will prepare the hearts of the people for the Word made flesh.

True in due season

Timing is everything, or so the saying goes. It is hard to overestimate the importance of doing something, or making a decision, at the right time. Even if the decision or plan of action is properly thought out, faulty timing can ruin the best laid plans. Of course proper timing is not something we achieve through a book or magic formula. There is a mysterious combination of perspiration and inspiration, hard work combined with creative imagination and a feel for the right time to act. A good investment is one which requires good timing. All athletic success and skill require good timing. Some of history's great battles and discoveries were the result of fortunate timing. Maybe timing isn't everything but it goes a long way in determining the success or failure of a goal.

We moderns have a problem with timing and things working out in due season. The reason for this difficulty is obvious. We don't like to wait. We demand instant results and immediate gratification. From instant foods to instant salvation, we expect everything to be delivered to us NOW! The Lord, however, does not deal with us according to our expectations.

In our Gospel reading the angel Gabriel's words to Zechariah will come true in due season. There is no rushing God's grace. The heart must be prepared. The inner depths of our being must be matured so that the Word will be planted on fertile ground and produce abundant fruit. In due season Elizabeth gives birth to John, the herald of the Messiah. In due season God will once again visit His people in the person of Jesus. Our hearts must be prepared to let the word be born in us. Hopeful patience is essential. We do not wait passively. We long for the word, knowing that in due season the One who is Light, Life, and Truth will come.

Reflection Questions. The grace of God is at work in us from the beginning of our existence. There is no moment when we are beyond the reach of God's grace. Samson is conceived by the grace of God and called to deliver Israel.

How does my daily work give praise to God?

_____
_____
_____
_____

How have I helped to protect unborn human life?

_____
_____
_____
_____

In what ways have I consecrated myself to the Lord?

_____
_____
_____
_____

The angel Gabriel announces that Zechariah and Elizabeth will give birth to a son. This child will be called John. Elizabeth gives praise to God for His grace. In seemingly impossible circumstances God brings forth new life.

What recent painful reproach has been removed by God's grace?

_____
_____
_____
_____
_____

MY ADVENT JOURNAL

Do I find myself looking for quick answers to my spiritual journey?

How have I shared my faith with children so they might know the Lord?

Closing Conversation. Spend a few minutes in quiet prayer. As Advent comes to a close reflect on your spiritual journey. Write your response below.

Gabriel: Tell me of an area of your spiritual life which seems lifeless. Pray that the Lord's grace will turn this dry place to one of abundance. Do you believe the Lord can do such a thing?

Response:

Novena
DECEMBER 20

Isaiah 7:10-14 The king of Israel during the prophecy of Isaiah is Ahaz. Unfortunately Ahaz lacks moral courage and a deep commitment to the covenant. The Lord will offer Ahaz a sign of his power: the virgin with child. The child will be called Emmanuel, "God is with us."

Luke 1:26-38 The angel Gabriel visits Mary and announces she will be the mother of Jesus. This will take place through the power of the Holy Spirit. Mary accepts the angel's message and places her total faith in God. Mary is the model Christian, and model for the Church, through her total surrender to the Word.

She was deeply troubled

In our Gospel reading from St. Luke we find these words about Mary: "She was deeply troubled by his (the angel Gabriel's) words, and wondered what his greeting meant." What St. Luke offers us is a picture of Mary which helps balance some of the more idealistic views of her. Mary is completely human. Even though she was spared the effects of original sin, she still knows our fears, joys, defeats, and victories that are part of being human. Her special place in salvation history does not remove her from the human condition. In fact, Mary reveals to us the pain and the joy of being human in a most profound manner.

We ought not forget that Mary was anxious, fearful, and deeply troubled over the words of Gabriel. This is important to remember because we have a tendency to think that faith leaves no room for doubt. However, a mature faith always must confront the reality of doubt. Daily we experience trials which cause us to question. We ought not suppress such doubts and feelings but bring them to God in trusting prayer. It is at the very places of our doubts that the grace of faith is made real and strong.

Mary's doubts and fears also remind us of one of the spiritual works of mercy, namely, bringing consolation to the troubled. The spiritual works of mercy must be joined with the corporal works of mercy so as to bring the healing ministry to the whole person. During this time of Advent and Christmas many experience loneliness and feel the absence of God. Many people lack the experience of peace and inner comfort. An essential call of the Christian life is bringing a word of encouragement. Like the angel Gabriel, we too can say, "Fear not, for the grace of God is yours. The Word is becoming flesh even now. The peace of Christ is yours. Open your heart to receive it."

MY ADVENT JOURNAL

Reflection Questions. Throughout the history of Israel Yahweh has given signs to His people. The wise are able to read the signs of the times. Yahweh is going to give a sign not only to Israel but all of humankind, namely, a virgin with child named Emmanuel: God with us.

Have I been wise in reading God's signs in my life for growing in holiness?

_____
_____
_____
_____

In what ways do I see God at work in our world today? List some current signs.

_____
_____
_____
_____

What are some of the ways in which our society is closed to God's signs?

_____
_____
_____
_____

The central figure in the birth of Jesus in the Gospel of Luke is Mary. She is a model of the Christian life. Mary is also the model for the Church. Both the individual Christian and the Church are to be servants of the Lord's word.

Have I grown spiritually through my prayer and study of Scripture?

_____
_____
_____
_____

DECEMBER 20

How has the Lord helped me through a hopeless situation?

Have I followed Mary's example by being a servant of the Lord's word? How?

Closing Conversation. Spend a few moments in prayerful reflection. Meditate on the Gospel reading. Write your response to Mary.

Mary: Tell me of a recent experience in which you were troubled by a spiritual challenge. How did God's grace strengthen you for the challenge?

Response:

Novena   DECEMBER 21

Song of Songs 2:8-14   To what shall we compare the love of God for His people? The romantic poet of Song of Songs compares God's love for us with the love between husband and wife. Separation is painful. New love speaks of spring when life bursts forth. God's love is life-giving and calls the people to turn from the winter of sin and death.

Luke 1:39-45   Mary rushes to be with Elizabeth who is pregnant with child. Mary is the woman for others. She knows that Elizabeth is in need of care. Mary forgets her own condition and role. All that matters to Mary is that she can be of service to someone in need.

Renew you in His love

Recent theology (David Tracy and Andrew Greeley) and not so recent theology (Song of Songs and St. Thomas), have focused on the importance of the religious imagination for the development of faith. To be specific, Catholics have an analogical religious imagination. That is, we Catholics believe that grace is everywhere and God is constantly revealing Himself to us through creation, relationships and daily experiences. Our understanding, or story, of God is such that we believe God is madly in love with us and wants us to respond to that divine passion.

More and more theologians are turning to story or narrative to help us understand and experience the boundless love of God. More and more we are being invited to look at our daily experiences to grow spiritually. And of special importance is the experience of marital love. The love of God for us is something like (analogous to) the intense, passionate, consuming, sacrificial and life-giving love between husband and wife. Of course, God loves us with infinitely greater intensity, but marital love offers us a special revelation of what God's divine love is like. Hence, we hold that marriage is a sacrament because of its power to reveal the divine at work in the thoroughly human. We come to know (experience) God by looking deeply into our humanity.

Advent brings together the deepest aspects of humanity: love, new life, commitment, integrity, faith, and hope in that which is beyond our present powers to understand. Mary, Joseph, and the child Jesus reveal to us the grace of God at work in our most intimate relationships as well as our deepest vows and loves. Advent is the time when we are renewed in God's love. It is a renewal that transforms the human heart and helps us to see everyday things with new eyes. Advent is God's offer to be renewed in love.

Reflection Questions. Too often we think of the Hebrew Scriptures as being totally irrelevant to modern concerns. Too often we have a picture of an angry God killing those who disobey. The Song of Songs is a beautiful spiritual poem about the power of human passion and God's passionate love for us.

How have I recently experienced God's passionate love?

What can the Church do to strengthen family life?

What are my most important commitments? How have I been faithful to them?

Mary is the model of the Christian life. She is totally open to receive God's Word and is a woman who gives herself in service to others. She teaches us that love of God always requires that we love our neighbor as we love ourselves. Mary shows us that Christian love is the giving of oneself to God and others.

In what ways have I volunteered my time and talents for my parish and city?

Have I become less self-centered and more other-directed? How?

_____
_____
_____
_____

How have I used my talents in order to make the world better for children?

_____
_____
_____
_____

Closing Conversation. Prayerfully read the Gospel account of Mary's going to visit Elizabeth. Write your response to Mary.

Mary: Tell me of a recent experience of spiritual joy you shared with a member of your family or a friend. How did such sharing help your joy to grow?

Response: _____
_____
_____
_____
_____
_____
_____
_____
_____
_____
_____
_____
_____

Novena

DECEMBER 22

1 Samuel 1:24-28 This selection recounts the dedication of Samuel to the Lord by his mother Hannah. Samuel's birth was in answer to Hannah's prayer. Hence, he is to be dedicated to the Lord and perform a special service for Yahweh. Life is a gift from God and we are to use this gift in praise of Him.

Luke 1:46-56 This selection from Luke's Gospel is called the Magnificat. It is a hymn of deepest thanksgiving by Mary in acknowledgment of all the great things the Lord has done. The Lord is mindful of His promises and the needs of His people. The Lord is about to act in a mighty show of love and deliverance.

Mary remained with Elizabeth

Our Gospel reading from St. Luke presents one of the great prayers of praise: Mary's Magnificat. In this hymn of praise Mary expresses her deepest gratitude to the Lord for the annunciation and the mighty deeds of deliverance throughout Israel's history; and for the fact that Yahweh acts on behalf of the poor and lowly. The Lord confronts the proud and reverses the fortunes of the self-satisfied and mighty. The poor of Yahweh will come to enjoy good things and hear good news.

The Magnificat is a beautiful prayer which acknowledges the mighty deeds of Yahweh. It is easy for us to get caught up in its splendor. What can be overlooked is the closing verse of our selection: "Mary remained with Elizabeth about three months and then returned home." We see in this subtle sentence a key insight into Mary's soul and a key aspect of Christian service.

Mary knows that the abundant grace of God has come to her in a special way. She will give God a human face. However, Mary goes in haste to be with Elizabeth. The mother of Jesus, the Messiah, goes to visit Elizabeth, the mother of John, the herald of her Son. Mary does not allow human convention to impede her joy. She must be with Elizabeth so as to share the joy of the Spirit and be of service. The joy which fills Mary's soul moves her to reach out to others as the Lord had reached out to her.

Also we see that Mary stayed with Elizabeth and then returned home. Mary strikes the perfect balance between being of service and allowing others to gain independence as we move on with our responsibilities. She doesn't stay beyond what is required. Ministry is helping others and empowering those we serve to develop their own talents and resources. Christian service is love in action, and a love which seeks to liberate.

84 MY ADVENT JOURNAL

Reflection Questions. The child Samuel was chosen by the Lord for a special work. His selection was totally the work of grace. Each of us has been chosen for a special work through Baptism. Each of us is dedicated to the Lord.

What special work has the Lord chosen for me?

_____
_____
_____

How have I accomplished this special work?

_____
_____
_____

In what ways has my family helped me in the Lord's work?

_____
_____
_____

One of the fruits of the indwelling of the Holy Spirit is joy. It is this joy in the Spirit which unites Mary and Elizabeth. They look at each other and know the Lord has abundantly blessed each with the gift of new life.

Have I helped empower others to know their God-given talents? Explain.

_____
_____
_____

Do I try to manipulate and control others by my service?

_____
_____
_____

DECEMBER 22

Do I love myself enough to care for my own needs as well as those of others?

Closing Reflections. Prayerfully read Mary's Magnificat. Next to the following aspects of the Magnificat write what they mean to you.

"My spirit finds joy in God, my Savior":

"God who is mighty has done great things for me":

"... ever mindful of His mercy":

"He has shown might with His arm":

Novena DECEMBER 23

Malachi 3:1-4, 23-24 The prophet Malachi announces the coming of the Messiah. Yet the Day of the Lord will also be a time of judgment and decision-making. With the coming of the Messiah we will have to make a declaration for or against the Messiah and the Kingdom of God.

Luke 1:57-66 St. Luke recounts the birth and naming of John the Baptizer. Contrary to human expectations the child will be called John which means, "Yahweh has shown favor." God has graced Elizabeth and Zechariah with a child in old age. This child will herald the Messiah.

Friendship with the Lord

"Show me your friends and I'll tell you who you are," is an often used expression when it comes to guiding the young in the selection of playmates. This expression, however, can serve us all well throughout our lives, for until we die we have the joyful and painful, exciting yet fearful task of choosing our friends. And we can never have too many friends. Of course friends are rare and acquaintances are many. Friendships are fragile and demand our constant attention and work. Friendships do not survive neglect.

The ancient Greek philosopher Aristotle accorded friendship a special place in the formation of character and the development of one's humanity. He taught that we can only be friends with our equals. Relationships that involve unequals (socially or economically) are not friendships in the real sense of the term. The reason for this is that Aristotle believed that mutuality was essential to friendship. There must be a balance between giving and receiving. Resentment results if one does all the giving or receiving. And only equals can reach this state of mutuality essential for friendship.

The Christian experience of friendship is radically different. The season of Advent tells us that we are friends of God through the birth of Jesus. Yes, friends of God! We poor, limited creatures are the friends of our Loving Creator. In fact, we are made in the very divine image and likeness of God. God, out of infinite love, created us and became one like us. In Jesus, the Word made flesh, we have been elevated into the very presence and family of God. Naturally we could never hope to be friends with God through our own merits or efforts. We are the friends of God through the free gift of Jesus. Advent calls us to be ready to receive the God who is our friend, and God enables us to be friends with one another.

Reflection Questions. The prophet Malachi asks a question which cuts to the very core of our souls: Who can endure the day of the Lord's coming? Only those who are purified by the cleansing word of the Lord.

Will I be able to endure the day of the Lord's coming?

How has reading the Scriptures turned my heart to the Lord?

How have I been a messenger of the Lord's coming during Advent?

It was the custom of the time to name the male child after the father or one of the family's great ancestors. However, this child is special. He will be called John. He is a favor (grace) given by Yahweh to Elizabeth and Zechariah. John is the messenger of the Messiah.

Who is my patron saint? How have I followed his/her example?

MY ADVENT JOURNAL

In what ways has the Holy Spirit helped me to proclaim God's word?

_____
_____
_____
_____

How has the Lord's mercy brought new life to the dead parts of my soul?

_____
_____
_____
_____

Closing Reflection. Spend a few moments in quiet reflection on friendship. Write a reflection on how your friendship with God has grown during Advent.

_____
_____
_____
_____

How have your human friendships helped you draw closer to Jesus?

_____
_____
_____
_____
_____

Novena
DECEMBER 24

2 Samuel 7:1-5, 8-11, 16 Human arrogance and pride know no limits. David is full of his own sense of accomplishment. What he has forgotten is that all belongs to the Lord and is the result of Yahweh's goodness. It is not David who will build a home for the Lord but the Lord who will establish David's dynasty forever.

Luke 1:67-79 This selection from St. Luke contains the beautiful Canticle of Zechariah. Under the inspiration of the Holy Spirit Zechariah praises God for the gift of his son John. The time of deliverance is near at hand. John is the final messenger preparing hearts for the Messiah.

The way of peace

These words, "the way of peace," bring Zechariah's Canticle to a close. This is most appropriate since life in the presence of God is peace. However the peace of God is not just any kind of peace. It is the peace only the Lord can give and the world can never take away. God's peace is not at the beginning of our journey in faith but at the end. Our hearts quicken with the thought of peace as we move further into Advent and closer to the words, "A Savior is born to us... Christ the Lord!" The temptation is always to grasp for an imitation of the Lord's peace.

We must keep ever before us the way that leads to the peace of the Lord. It is a way that involves us deeply in the cost of discipleship. It cost God something to take on our poor human flesh and become one of us in Jesus. It cost Jesus something to accept the Cross on our behalf so we might have the hope of eternal life. It continues to cost God something as the Spirit abides with us in human history. The way of peace, and the commitment to love, always travels down the road which demands we give ourselves.

Today we prepare our hearts for the birth of the Messiah. He is the One who is our peace and our hope of glory. Our hearts are filled with joy and eager expectation of the One who is lasting peace. However, the One who is our peace is born in a stable. There is no room in the inn of a world which tries to find peace through its own design. Yet our hearts cannot be contained, for deep inside we keep vigil in hopeful anticipation of the One who is our peace; our lasting peace.

Reflection Questions. All that we have, are, and hope to be results from the abundant grace of God. We easily forget this. We often believe that success and achievement are the sole work of our efforts. The prophet Nathan reminds King David (and each of us) that everything belongs to the Lord.

What achievements and successes do I take great pride in?

_____
_____
_____
_____

Do I give God praise for all His gifts to me? How?

_____
_____
_____
_____

In what ways have I shared my gifts with others to the praise of God?

_____
_____
_____
_____

The silence of Zechariah is turned to a hymn of praise. The birth of John brings us closer to the Messiah. The Lord has acted to rescue His people from sin and death. John the Baptizer will play a significant role as herald.

How has silent prayer and meditation helped me to draw close to Jesus?

_____
_____
_____
_____

How have I walked in the way of God's peace during Advent?

How have I been open to speak the prophetic words of the Holy Spirit?

Closing Reflection. Prayerfully read the Canticle of Zechariah. In the space below write your own canticle or hymn of praise to the Lord for His graces to you during this Advent season.

Jesus: The Word Made Flesh

In the Prologue of John's Gospel we are invited into the upper realms of spiritual reality. Namely, we are given a glimpse of the Eternal Word who is Light and Truth. This Eternal Word was in the presence of God, and is God. The eternal Word brought all things into existence and is the power which keeps all things in place. The majesty and splendor of the Word is beyond our poor powers of comprehension. Yet in verse 14 of the Prologue we are confronted with the deepest of mysteries and the deepest expression of God's love and commitment to us: "The Word became flesh and dwelt among us."

These words about the Word escape our powers to understand and indicate our limits to express the inexpressible. However, one thing is clear: through the Word becoming flesh in Jesus, God has committed himself forever to our cause. God will never turn away from us or reject us. The Word spoken into the darkness of the long night of our soul's captivity proclaims a freedom, acceptance, and love which drives out all fear. The Word made flesh speaks to us of the Good News of our salvation. The mortal enemies of our hope — sin and death — will not have the last word. There is a Light which shines in the darkness and is not overcome. There is a Word which became our flesh so that we might become fully human and alive to the praise of God in the Spirit.

Throughout this Advent season we have been engaged in the joyful, yet tension-filled, task of preparing ourselves for the birth of Jesus. Today the fruits of our preparation are to yield a harvest: a harvest rich in the Spirit of peace, love, joy, kindness, meekness, and compassion. This harvest is anything but a one day bonanza. The harvest of the Spirit is one that is to grow and mature throughout the course of a lifetime. Today, with its harvest in the Spirit, is not a Christmas gift that we use for a week and then move on to something else. The gifts of the Spirit, and the abiding meaning of this season, are to be used and shared until we see our Lord face to face.

Advent is a time of preparation for the birth of our Savior. The Word has become flesh in our history, and hopefully in our hearts. But we also live each day in Advent time. We daily prepare ourselves for that final coming when the Lord will call us home to that eternal banquet in the Kingdom. The very same Lord who became our flesh will come again. It is always Advent for the Christian. We are always waiting for the Lord to come, and come again. In our celebration of the Eucharist we say, "... Christ will come again." May He find us ready. May He find us eager and joyful. When the Lord comes again, may there be abundant room in the inn of our hearts to receive Him.

Closing Reflection. Spend some quiet, prayerful time reflecting on this past Advent season. Write your reflections on the ways in which the Word has become flesh in your life. Reflect on those experiences which have helped you to draw closer to Jesus our Savior.

Advent notes and thoughts

Advent notes and thoughts

Advent notes and thoughts

Advent notes and thoughts